D1502964

MONDAY
THROUGH
SATURDAY

MONDAY
THROUGH
SATURDAY

From the Heart, ™

JOYCE
LANDORF

WORD BOOKS
PUBLISHER
WACO, TEXAS

A DIVISION OF
WORD, INCORPORATED

MONDAY THROUGH SATURDAY

Copyright © 1984 by Joyce Landorf

Library of Congress Cataloging in Publication Data

Landorf, Joyce.
  Monday through Saturday.

  (From the heart)
    1. Christian life—1960–   I. Title.   II. Series:
Landorf, Joyce. From the heart.
BV4501.2.L31824   1984   248.4   84–23459
  ISBN 0–8499–0380–7

Scripture quotations used in this book are from the following versions:
    The Living Bible (TLB), copyright © 1971 by Tyndale House Publishers, Wheaton, IL.
    The Revised Standard Version of the Bible (RSV), copyright © 1946, 1952 © 1971 and 1973 by the Division of Christian Education of the National Council of the Churches of Christ in the U.S.A.

Printed in the United States

♥

It's Monday, but let me tell you about yesterday. Sunday! What a day!

The brilliant sunshine, the cloudless expanse of sky, and the bachelor-button blue sea with its endless supply of frothy white surf was a breathless sight—picture perfect.

The spirit of high expectations outside and inside our church sanctuary was at once both warm and homey, yet regal and majestic. It was God's presence, our attendance, the opening prayer, the beauty of the powerful music, the greetings of others around us, the sharing in the offering, our pastor's sermon on missionaries, even our visit with friends to the donut shop after the service that made Sunday a high and holy day. We were filled with godly excitement, and we drove home having had our minds stretched, our hearts enlarged, and our dedication to bringing Christ to lonely and broken souls firmly established and warmly rekindled in our hearts.

But that was yesterday. Today it's Monday.

Now I must leave the warm cocoon of Sunday. I must leave the house of God and His people to take up daily residence in the cold world of Monday through Saturday.

Almost eighty years ago, Charles Reynolds Brown published a study book of Job. How strange it is that his words written so long ago could reach out and touch today's Monday. But they do. He writes,

> The book of Job has stood for generations as one of the great dramas of doubt. . . . We find a certain man of unblemished integrity in the full enjoyment of health, property, family joy, and a life of kindly usefulness, brought to the point where he feels the foundations slipping from under him because of the terrible misfortunes which the God of righteousness allows to fall upon his home of peace. It is, therefore, not a clever contest between two hair-splitting theories, but a battle of warm faith with hard cold facts, that we find portrayed in the book of Job.

Then, this visionary man writes of the Christians who lived in the early 1900s saying,

> It is at this very point that the busy people of the world today most commonly find themselves puzzled. They listen on Sunday to the warm assurances of faith put forth from the pulpits of the land. . . . A God who knows that we have need of all things that are demanded for joyous and useful experience; a Friend who does not suffer even a sparrow to fall to the ground without His notice; a Father who is more ready to hear and answer the prayerful appeals of His people than earthly fathers are to give bread to

their children; an Allembracing Providence whose affectionate interest in our well-being counts the very hairs on our heads! Then on Monday morning they go out into the world . . . not some imaginary world as men have agreed together to picture it to themselves, but the real world as it is. They rub against the un-planed side of it and find it rough, full of knots and splinters. They are torn and bruised by the contact; or, if happily they themselves escape for a time, they painfully witness the discomfiture of their less fortunate fellows. They ponder the apparent discrepancies between the warm theories of the pulpit and the cold facts which face them.

Well said, dear man of yesteryear. You have succinctly described Christians' conflicts in the past between warm faith and cold facts. We who live now—in the present—are no different. We leave the warmth of God's house and the ardent encouragement of balcony people on Sunday, only to face the chilling reality of Monday in our homes, our jobs, or in our relationships of this world.

I write this book as an attempt to bridge the gap from one Sunday to another . . . to bring us all some reality, some helpful ways to cope, and some practical concepts for our journey Monday through Saturday. In short, I pray this bridge will assuage your doubts, calm your fears, and give you a measure of hope when it comes to dealing with the cold facts of daily living. But if these words are to bridge the gap, then we must start by defining biblically, practically, and constructively what makes Christians warm and real, and what kind of living theology carries us from Monday to Saturday.

Real Christians know
that real love remembers
the sweet missives,
the phone calls,
the tiny gifts of love . . .

But they also know that
real love does not need
to keep a scoreboard.

Often the stress points of my life have been so draining I am dry—"peopled-out"—and the ability to smile, to listen, or to give one more hug is there—but just barely. It is in these moments that the Lord sends someone along to express or give love in a very healing, restorative way. For instance,

- ♥ A ministering letter from my pastor John.

- ♥ A look of total comprehension from my daughter-in-law Teresa.

- ♥ A letter or a box of butterfly stationery from my daughter Laurie.

- ♥ A prayer offered over the phone by my friend Mac.

- ♥ A dish of gardenias grown and picked by my husband Dick.

- ♥ A soft but poignant sentence spoken by my friend and associate Joann.

- ♥ A balcony person's cheer from my long-time friend and representative Von.

- ♥ A delicate urging to read aloud what I've just written from my publisher Francis or my editor Beverly.

All of these things and more are remembered, but never with the idea of who's done what or whose turn it is to give. Love remembers but doesn't keep score, for sometimes we cannot do or give—we can only sit back and receive.

*Real Christians
know that to be
spiritually outspoken
with ever-ready
solutions and answers
is of great value
like highly polished
sterling silver.*

*But to be spiritually mute
or to confess, "Honestly,
I don't know,"
is more often the
better choice
and valued like
burnished gold.*

I honestly don't have a whole lot of answers. But by virtue of my books, tapes, speaking, films, and broadcasting—I am *expected,* as a Christian leader, to expound on all subjects, and give answers and solutions. Even Sunday school teachers are supposed to sound practically omnipotent.

Yet in my own personal life, when I was *beyond* desperate for answers, the most healing words came from a dear pastor friend of mine who looked me in the eye and said, "Joyce, I don't know!"

Sometimes there simply *are* no answers. More often there are possible exceptions, modifications, and things I cannot logically explain.

Since when is it close to sinning when a Christian says to another Christian, "I don't know what God is doing!" Some situations defy deciphering. Some tragedies stubbornly refuse all explanations. And sometimes only *God* knows the ultimate alternative.

I need to appreciate the delicate balance between the silver of wise speech and the gold of honest and sometimes merciful silence, if I am to be *truly* used of God.

*Real Christians know
that the journey on the
road toward health,
wealth, and happiness
is sometimes in the
opposite direction
from "Take up thy cross
and follow Me."*

Where did we ever get the notion that joy and suffering are *not* two parts of the same package? How can we state in so many ways the fallacy that God's children *always* become healthy, wealthy, and miraculously wise?

We never learned this from our studies of Abraham, Isaac, Jacob, Rachel, Joseph, Moses, Jochebed, Miriam, Joshua, David, Abigail, Elijah, Job, Isaiah, Daniel, or Habakkuk—to name just a few from the Old Testament alone.

Why do we teach our children the half-truth that if they accept Christ they will have a glorious life after death, and that life right now will be one *pain-free,* joyous experience after another?

When will we truly read and absorb the Word of God into our bloodstreams and understand that we need to teach our children about the precious ointment of joy which often is purchased at the high cost of suffering and sacrifice. Christ's resurrection was preceded by His death. Oh, how we need to teach that life brings both pain and joy; and, though the suffering is real, still it is *temporary* and will ultimately be forgotten. But the joy, oh, the joy lasts forever!

*Real Christians understand
the great importance of
expressing ruth to one another
especially in the home . . .*

*For if our partners,
our children,
or we ourselves
do not find ruth at home,
it is pretty certain that
we will not find it in the
cold, ruthless world
outside the home.*

*Real Christians live such
honest and caring lives
that when death takes
them home to God,
we mourn our loss and
miss them immeasurably.*

My dictionary defines the word *ruth* as an emotional feeling such as pity, tenderness, sorrow, grief, or remorse. The exact opposite of ruthless.

Often I find an appalling lack of ruth in my own life and in the lives of others. It seems easier to strike back, to lash out, than to cultivate the ambience of ruth.

Recently a father asked, "How can my kids be so protective and loving to each other one minute, and so downright mean to each other the next?" His question made me remember the kind/mean syndrome of my children. *Chalk it up to sibling rivalry,* I thought. *But, is it more than that? Is it the absence of ruth?*

If I am going to teach myself and my family about the feelings of tenderness, sorrow, and remorse, then I need to start listening with a tenderness of heart, I need to have a flexible attitude and an understanding of my own suffering, and I need to own my responsibilities—graciously taking the credit when I'm wrong.

I do not want to be known as ruthless, for it is as Christless as possible.

It is not wrong to mourn or to miss those we have loved when death carries them to God.

It *is* wrong to assume that because we will see them again someday in heaven that our knowledge takes away our inner pain.

The fact that Vera is in her heavenly home with God does not ease the loneliness of the moment when Cy walks into their earthly home each night after work. It is no wonder that when I ask how long Vera has been gone Cy answers instantly, "Ten months and three days." And then he tells me that the ache is even greater now than at the time of her death. Puzzled, he asks me why.

Have we brainwashed ourselves into a death denial which leads us to believe that because a person died *in Christ,* we who are left will experience no grief, no despair, or no bereavement?

On the contrary, real Christians are a rare minority breed; and, when one dies, we experience a strange mixture of despair and hope—despair because we miss them so . . . and hope because ultimately we will see them again. But let's not forget that despair *and* hope are part of the same package.

It is valid to mourn and to miss them. It is equally valid to hope.

Real Christians
hold a young
woman's hand
after she has
just miscarried
and do not
say a word.

"It was *just* a miscarriage," says an insensitive aunt.

"Hey, no big deal," a young husband comments as he shrugs his shoulders.

"Snap out of this and get on with living," a mother who has never experienced a miscarriage commands.

"You're making too much over this, all you want is sympathy," admonishes a pastor, without sound understanding or a sense of compassion.

Oh, what damage our tongue and vocal cords can inflict in the name of "helping" someone through a difficult crisis.

Nothing comforts, heals, or steadies the hurting heart quite as much as the love of God pouring through the hand—*not the voice*—of a brother or sister in Christ.

When Jesus was here His words were powerful, true; but often, it was *His touch that healed.*

Listen to the whisperings of the Holy Spirit the next time a woman you know has a miscarriage, or loses an infant; and then, in God's name, reach out and hold her tenderly in your arms of unconditional love and your heart of constant prayers.

*A real Christian
knows that merely
listening to someone
is not enough . . .*

*It takes listening
between the words
to really hear
what's being said.*

Two aisles over in the K-Mart store the man from our church waved a "hello" at me. Then we had the following exchange:

"How are you, Joyce?"

"Fine." (At this point he was not asking—merely greeting, and there is a difference.)

"How's the jaw pain?" (*Now* he's asking.)

"Well, to be honest, it's a little worse today."

"Praise the Lord! I'm glad you're doing so well."

Huh? I just stood there between the racks of baby clothes and the boy's section, smiling and shaking my head. Why didn't I just lie and tell him I had no pain? That's what he wanted to hear. Aren't *true* Christians *always* victorious, wealthy, and completely pain-free?

No, certainly not. And when we ask someone specifically how they are doing, we must do two things: (1) give them the freedom to *honestly tell us,* and (2) be willing to listen closely to what's being said and what's *not* being said.

What do the eyes say? Is there a droop in the shoulders as well as the timbre of their voice? Did they answer eagerly or reluctantly? How can we "bear one another's burdens" if we do not listen between the words? Jesus said, "A new commandment I give you . . . love one another."

*Real Christians
look for practical
ways to be
balcony people
to others.*

*Even on a mean,
malignant Monday
or a wild,
weird Wednesday
or a fragile
yet frantic Friday,
their love finds
ways to help us
wait for the
coming of Sunday.*

One woman, after being a balcony person to another woman for almost twenty years, continually seeks ways to cheer her friend on. Here is the latest letter in her efforts.

In case you have any "basement people" in your life today, I just want you to know I'm in your balcony. Here are a few things I love about you after my seventeen-and-a-half-year study!

1. You go way out of your way to show love.

2. You are not a phony . . . and you've helped me to see through phonies and helped me be more conscious when I tend to become that way.

3. You make everyone you come in contact with feel "special"!

4. You make me feel lovely . . . even when I feel *most* unlovely.

5. You nurture my sense of humor, and you don't think it's weird to laugh at some weird things.

6. You instill in me a desire to be better and better. Sometimes you make me feel I *am* better than I think I am.

7. You have chosen me to be a part of your life—and have given me a friendship which has upheld me through thick and thin.

8. You are just really a REAL person, fun-loving, close to the Lord, honest, and even when things are very bad—you are special.

What a letter for Monday through Saturday!

*Real Christians
know that their
daily walk
in Christ
is best reflected
in being and
doing . . .
not in the phrasing
and wording
of their talk.*

I wish the world around us had a magic way of seeing the genuine commitment of our inner hearts to God.

I wish people could see the time spent in prayer . . . the preparations that go into sermons, Sunday school lessons, and choir rehearsals . . . the tithes cheerfully given . . . the private solitude of study and the reading of God's Word. In short, I wish the world could always see the *intent* of our hearts.

But alas! All the world really knows of us and our claim to faith is what they see. Consider this, the world most generally sees us impatient and critical in the grocery store, frustrated by prices at the gas pumps, hostile or unapproachable during a crisis at the job or in an office situation, and downright unreasonable or oblivious to others on the highways and our city streets.

The lost people around us will never really hear the Good News of Christ when we tell them, unless our lives, our actions, and our responses clearly *show* that knowing the Lord does, indeed, make all the difference.

Today I need to remember: My words are usually superseded by my actions—and then live accordingly.

*Real Christians
know that sometimes
the only way
the world around us
will ever see Christ
is through the
fiery flames of
our own trials
and suffering.*

My sister, Marilyn Hontz, had been reading the oft-told story of the Hebrew men who were thrown into the fiery furnace by King Nebuchadnezzar (Daniel, chapter 3, TLB). Suddenly she saw something she'd not seen before, thought of my struggle with pain, and phoned me.

Breathlessly she read, " 'But suddenly, as he was watching, Nebuchadnezzar jumped up in amazement and exclaimed to his advisors, "Didn't we throw three men into the furnace?"

" ' "Yes," they said, "we did indeed, Your Majesty."

" ' "Well, look!" Nebuchadnezzar shouted. "I see *four* men, unbound, walking around in the fire and they aren't even hurt by the flames! And the fourth looks like a god!" ' "

Marilyn paused and said, "Oh, Joyce, just think, the king would have *never* seen the Lord had the men not been in the furnace. Maybe the furnace of your pain is the only place others will really see Jesus. . . ."

I am filled with a new appreciation of the furnace. Perhaps the fiery experience is twofold: to refine us into the purest of gold and to let others catch their first (and possibly their only) look at Jesus.

Maybe I can stay in the furnace a little longer. Are you game to stay too?

*Real Christians
know that God is
able to deliver
them . . .*

*But they also know
that even if He doesn't
deliver them today,
ultimately He will!*

Do I really believe God is able? These three men did, and they had absolutely no guarantees! Listen to them:

Shadrach, Meshach, and Abednego replied, "O Nebuchad-nezzar, we are not worried about what will happen to us. If we are thrown into the flaming furnace, *our God is able to deliver us;* and he will deliver us out of your hand, Your Majesty. But if he doesn't, please understand, sir, that even then we will never under any circumstances serve your gods or worship the golden statue you have erected (Daniel 3:16–18, TLB, emphasis mine).

Not long ago when my T.M.J. (temporomandibular joint stress dysfunction) pain was at level four, I asked two friends of mine if "God was able." They assured me that God was indeed able. Later one friend wrote, "God is able . . . when it seems like you're all alone, when it seems like everything is against you, when it seems like everyone else is winning, except you, when you're so discouraged that you almost don't care any-more. Yes, God is able to use your victories and your failures, to use your strengths and your weaknesses, to turn your dreams to plans, and your plans into fruition, to work through *your* love when everything else does not seem to be enough. Yes, He is able!"

*Real Christians
see spring's
first daffodil
and believe
all the more in
life after death.*

It's easy to get all bogged down with the heat of summer,
  the frantic pace of change in the coming of autumn,
  the cold gripping freeze of winter, and
  miss the daffodils, the hope of spring.

Sometimes the pain or the stress of the seasons of life
block out my ability to reason,
  to remember, and
  even to recall the blessed fact that someday
  spring's first daffodils will bloom, and once again
  I'll be enchanted with life.

Oh, Lord, restore to me the joy of my salvation. Help me to look above the greyish-brown clay I'm made of, up to the pale yellow daffodils of Your mercy and grace. Help me also to remember the words from the old spiritual "Deep River," for they enable me to have the hope of looking forward to spring!

Oh chillun, don't you want to go to that gospel feast,
That promised land, that land where all is peace,
Walk into heaven and take my seat
And cast my crown at Jesus' feet?

Deep river, my home is over Jordan,
Deep river, Lord,
I want to cross over into campground.

Real Christians
know that
Dark Thoughts
can rain on
their parade.

But they have
the umbrella
of choice
to shelter them
as they march.

What if my child has a life-threatening accident? What if I lose my job? What if my marriage is destroyed? What if the lump is malignant?

These scary "what-if" questions hound us from time to time. I call them Dark Thoughts.

Right now the Dark Thoughts of my life which nag me during the day and give me insomnia at night can produce even darker fears. Intellectually I know the fears are false. Emotionally I feel devastated. But spiritually I understand I have a choice.

I can expose the Dark Thoughts for exactly what they are: tragedies that haven't yet happened. And I can choose to let that knowledge control my responses to those thoughts. In fact, when the Dark Thoughts do actually become reality, then God will give me the grace I need to deal with them. Until then, I choose to give them no quarter of my mind. I refuse to let them rule my life. I refuse to let them cripple my spirit.

I choose to slip under the umbrella of choice to call those Dark Thoughts false and to get on with the parade of life with confidence.

*Real Christians
endure many things
they do not begin
to understand . . .
because they
really see
and believe
a God who does
understand.*

In the early 1900s, Charles Reynolds Brown wrote these pertinent, amazingly contemporary lines about Christians' understanding of present events.

> It is true to this hour that the strength of any life to do, to bear, to hold fast its course, will be in proportion to the fullness and clearness of its vision of God . . . [Christians] are sorely puzzled to know how all these inexplicable things are working together for good, but they see God and confide in Him.

It seems to me that enduring, bearing, and holding fast are as rare as ancient art . . . except on the days when I stop trying to solve all the puzzles, when I refrain from giving God the finer points of my solutions, and when I simply rest in seeing and believing Him.

It sounds simple when I write it down, doesn't it? Yet, a healthy faith based on a positive God-concept is very definitely what makes "enduring" possible . . . even when we understand little or nothing of our circumstances.

*Real Christians have
learned that prayers
laced with healthy faith
are not presumptuous,
audacious, or arrogant . . .*

*Instead, they are based
on love of the Father,
needs of our own humanity,
and a willingness to accept
God's timetable.*

"Humbly," my mother said, "humbly, with the eager heart of a child, we tiptoe into God's throneroom and prayerfully petition Him. *Never* do we barge in, demanding this and that of God!"

Some of us have become so spiritually haughty we stamp our feet, demand our rights, and, pointing to a verse of Scripture, we shout, "I've *claimed* this, so God *has got* to honor it . . ."

We do indeed, barge into God's throneroom, give Him instructions as to how He is to answer and when He is to do our bidding, and end up reminding Him of *His* commitment to us! (As if He is under some kind of obligation to us that He has forgotten!)

My friend Chuck Swindoll, in discussing prayer in his great *Insights* magazine, wrote, "Faith does not mean we give God deadlines." A healthy faith produces prayers that are humble, loving, truthful, and that above all are not presumptuous, but dedicated to waiting.

In His time, He makes all things beautiful.

Real Christians
do the dishes,
bring over a meal, and
give unconditional support
to a grief-stricken family
instead of saying,
"If there's anything
I can do, call me."

I remember . . .

My family doctor silently holding my hands after our infant son died.

I remember . . .

My daughter sitting on the couch beside me, with her own stack of Kleenex just for crying with me.

I remember . . .

A friend's light kiss on the back of my neck at my mother's funeral.

I remember . . .

My grandfather's death and holding my sobbing grandmother while she wailed, "Papa, vy you go and not take me?"

I remember . . .

The friend who came and cleaned the bathrooms and my kitchen months after my mother's funeral.

It seems to me real Christians rarely say, "If there's anything I can do. . . ." They just do it!!

Real Christians
know that,
when comforting
a grieving person,
the best form
of ministering
is often just
plain old-fashioned
hugging and crying
together.

If there was one message I'd like to bring from the hearts of those who mourn to the hearts of those who would comfort, it would be this:

Say as *little* as possible, and *do* as *much* as possible.

Somehow we have translated the word *comfort* to mean the giving of words, verbal solutions, and timely sermons. But in reality it means practical, silent giving of ourselves, being there, and doing small and large tasks.

When told that one of his best friends had died, Jesus *said* nothing. He wept.

Perhaps weeping, holding, giving to needs, and doing the tasks that need to be done is the true measure of our ability to comfort at Jesus' level.

It's funny, but when I was in mourning for our son, my grandfather, and my mother, I remember the *acts* of comfort by others . . . but I've forgotten all their words.

*Real Christians
understand that arguing
divides families,
destroys relationships,
kindles fires of destruction,
and closes the very doors
that may have opened for a
better understanding
between people.*

I love the line in the last act in the drama of Job that reads, "Then, when Job prayed for his friends, the Lord restored his wealth and happiness" (42:10, TLB).

Job's three friends had been miserable comforters. They rubbed salt and vinegar into his open sores, they flogged him with the clubs of their dogma, they brazenly accused him of secret sins and wickedness, and they hammered away at his integrity.

Job stoutly and steadfastly argued his case with them to no avail. The heated pleadings did no good, nor did anything change. However, when Job's heart went out in loving compassion to his stiff-necked, blind, and ignorant friends, it was *then* that restoration and wholeness came to this weary, suffering man.

Lord, write this lesson on my suffering heart today.

*Real Christians
know they have
the freedom
to see or read
whatever they want . . .
But sometimes they
choose not to.*

The accusation "The church is full of hypocrites" is not very acceptable to most of us who really love the Lord. But nonetheless this cloud of criticism has always hovered over believers. And it still does.

Perhaps we brag too much about our spiritual prowess, lording it over the "publicans and sinners" in our world. Maybe when a nonbeliever finds out about our heavenly connections he or she scrutinizes our daily dealings and we come up *very* wanting.

The personal level of our integrity, and our reluctance to own the responsibility for our actions, often destroys our credibility. The world then labels us "phony," and what testimony we'd like to share is invalidated by the contrast between our words and the life we lead.

Twice this past week I verbalized and acted out a very hypocritical thing. I am deeply convicted. Am I one of the prime and visible examples of hypocrites who fill our churches?

O Lord, help!

*Real Christians know
that accepting Christ
into their hearts
is the easiest
(sometimes the only)
thing to do . . .*

*Being a living example
every day from then on
is the hard part.*

My grocery cart was in front of hers at the checkout stand. The enormous mound in her basket matched mine in volume and accumulated time, so I shot her a knowing glance and said, "My, are we having fun, or are we having fun?"

"Yes," she laughed. "But do you realize the worst is yet to come?"

I thought she meant paying for it, but she added, "Now we have to go home, put it all away, and then get it all out again each day to cook it."

True. The easy part is shopping and making the choices. The hard part was yet to come.

For many of us, coming to Christ was the ultimate necessity of life. We *chose* to open the door of our heart to God. Some of us think that *choice* was all there was to it. But not so. Now there is the daily living, the walking with Christ, the caring for others, and the continual process of taking up our cross.

If I want to survive physically I will have to buy food, bring it home, and prepare it. Help me Lord, not to be weary of the spiritual choice I have made, nor of the process it requires; for they stretch my soul to its maximum potential.

*Real Christians know
that spectacular,
instantaneous,
Cecil B. DeMille-type
miracles are possible . . .*

*But they happen most often
only in the movies.*

I am not talking about the word *censorship,* but rather the word *choice.*

When it comes to books and television I believe, because I am an adult Christian woman, that my power of choice is enormous. I am in charge of the choices in my life.

I do not agree with some young mothers I know who will not allow their children to see a certain children's TV program. (I think the show is entertaining *and* incredibly educating.) But I will defend, until I die, the right of those mothers to *choose.* This is a beautiful freedom we have before God.

I love the principle Paul lays down in 1 Corinthians 10:23 when he says, " 'All things are lawful,' but not all things are helpful. 'All things are lawful,' but not all things build up" (RSV). His words speak to my ability to choose and the responsibility that goes along with that freedom.

Real Christians
sense that
our world
will somehow
be changed for
the better . . .
because of what
God will do
through them.

I used to think that the poetic words, "God has brought you to the kingdom for just such a time as this," were the exclusive property of beautiful Queen Esther. But that puts both God and Esther in a box . . . and I'm trying to cut that out!

The God I worship and love is totally unlimited in His creative ability. The ingenious plans that God has for *each of us* are truly mind-boggling.

The world *will* be better, the light of truth *will* shine brighter, and the hope in the midst of despair *will* dawn on the lost of every generation, because of God at work in you . . . and me.

We don't have to lament the fact that we women are not the beautiful Queen Esther, or that you men are not the handsome King David. No, we are ourselves, designed in God's image— His chosen children!

We can change our world by allowing God the freedom to work out His plan. And we can leave ourselves open to God's creative ways without either one of us being boxed in.

Real Christians
are not so
preoccupied with
enjoying the freedom
of God's peace,
prosperity,
or patience
that they overlook
their responsibilities
to live godly,
yes, even holy,
lives of integrity.

I find that a few Christian slang phrases go a long way. I am not talking of the person who sincerely says "God bless you" or asks "How are you doing?" But I *am* weary of the trite, overworked small talk in which many of us engage.

The verbal exchange that touches me at my deepest level is the one that says, "Joyce, I'm holding you up daily before the Lord, and I'm asking Him to give you the strength you need."

Nothing trite here—only a caring heart, a person implementing the scripture "Bear ye one another's burdens" without meddling or prying and without exercising insensitive triteness.

How beautiful to know two or three Christians who understand how to be balcony people—people who know how to just be there when we desperately need them, yet most of all, people who by their conversation demonstrate that they are not merely being polite or making small talk, but that they care enough to involve themselves in our lives!

How beautiful are their words . . .

Real Christians
never underestimate
the affirmative power
of standing together
nor the healing power
of gentling one another.

"Kiss Mama Joy gently, and *don't hurt her jaw!*" Laurie's admonition caught my three-and-a-half-year-old grandson in midair.

Abruptly, he shifted gears just short of delivering the customary neck-breaking hug and intense smack, then announced, "I'll give her a gentleman's kiss." Lifting my hand with elegance, he bestowed upon it a very gentle kiss.

I was surprised and *most* impressed.

How sweet James's kiss felt on my hand. How dear of my daughter to know that, even though my head was aching, I still wanted to be hugged and kissed by her little son. He is young yet, but James is being taught the true value of *standing* with someone you love and the nearly lost art of gentling others.

When we are really hurting, the last thing we need is *more hurt*—either the physical hurt of bumping, jostling, or some other trauma . . . or the emotional hurt of someone lecturing or judging us. The first thing we need is for someone to *stand* with us—and then to gentle us.

I asked James to marry me.

Real Christians know
that spending time
in God's waiting room
is a perfectly normal
experience.

The joy comes
in understanding
that we do not
wait alone and
that waiting is
only a temporary
experience.

When the earthfilled Teton dam broke in Idaho a few years back, our friends the Bauers lost virtually everything. The immense flood swallowed up and swept away homes, farms, and whole towns.

In a letter to me, Clare Bauer wrote about the period of waiting which followed the water's devastation. In one part she commented,

> The one thing we *can* count on is that we are not alone. God *will* supply whatever we need.
>
> However, there is sometimes a time-lag between our knowing that and experiencing it—so occasionally we are put in what seems to be an endless holding pattern. But God will never fail us. He cannot.

How right she was to call my attention to a time-lag. Lord, forgive me for being impatient with Your time frame; and let me experience a quiet joy in just the *waiting on You.*

*Real Christians know
they don't have to be
strong, fearless,
and victorious
all the time
because they have a
Savior who is!*

In the weeks after the flood, while Clare and Conn Bauer were assessing the damage and trying to put some semblance of order back into their lives, Clare wrote of her frustrations, her tears, and her losses. I'll never forget her words.

Joyce, how blessed it is to have the freedom in Christ to cry and to feel broken whenever you suffer a loss!

How wonderful to know that just because we are Christians we don't have to be strong *all the time*—because we have a Savior who is!

On the days when I've felt the weakest, the most broken, and the waves of depression are the strongest, it *is* wonderful to know that it's all right! I'm not a bad, weak, or defeated Christian . . . but rather, I can take my brokenness to the Lord—and His wholeness can be mine.

I don't need to be strong all the time.

Real Christians
know that every good
relationship,
every child that
God gives us,
and all our
material possessions
are to be held
with open arms . . .

God's people
can afford to let go,
for, in the final analysis,
we are the richest people
in the world.

The realization of the great extent of her losses from the devastating flood was an annihilating experience for Clare. She discovered that the things she valued the most were photo albums with baby pictures, wedding pictures, and snapshots recording over twenty-five years of marriage. Gone too were the stitcheries she had made and all the handmade gifts her four daughters and one son had given at birthdays and Christmas.

Clare wrote,

> There is no way to put a value on those things, and perhaps I shouldn't—but I did and *I still do!*
>
> Our lives, you see, do not consist of just this *one* day. They are a composite of all our days, and so many of those lost objects were really a part of me. I grieved for those losses terribly.
>
> But in the months following the flood, God allowed me to see that I could *afford* to let go of them. That lesson was the most important one I was to learn from the whole experience.

Hold every thing and every person with open arms; for as God's people, we are wealthy beyond all human expectations.

*Real Christians
are not overly
preoccupied
with what has
been harvested.*

*But they are
clearly committed
to the fields
which remain
to be harvested.*

I've always had the mistaken idea that a missionary is some-one who leaves home to take the Good News of Christ to a foreign land.

"Not so," says my pastor, John Maxwell. "Missionaries go where people are hurting and where there are people in need."

In other words, the true definition of a missionary is *anyone* who leaves the parameters of his or her home, finds someone who is hurting and in need, and brings that person to God. We are *all* missionaries in that sense, and geographically our mission field is anywhere—that's Africa, China, or even our own backyard.

The harvest is all around us. The need is all around us. The hurting and lost are all around us. Come, let's go to the mission field together! Let's not sit back and excuse ourselves by saying, "I'm not *called* to be a missionary." No . . . wherever there are hurting people the harvest waits, ready for people of faith to be committed to Christ enough to harvest it.

*Real Christians
know about the
disillusioning
battles fought
between their warm
Sunday faith
and the cold
Monday facts . . .
But they choose
to endure the war.*

Enduring is the name of the game—not muddling mindlessly through life, hoping we'll be able to hang on, but enduring in joy. Teilhard de Chardin, the French mystic, said, "Joy is not the absence of pain but the presence of God."

Perhaps if we reexamined our God-concept and realized that *He really is able* to give us solutions to the wars we fight; and perhaps if we understood more of God's ways and the obstacles *we* place in His path; then, maybe then, we'd endure with a measure of God's joy! We'd be *alive* with His presence.

God is *more* than able to deliver us from our enemies, you know. And, as a friend of mine wrote,

> Faith, like life itself, is a process that develops from experience to experience, from crisis to crisis, day to day, and year to year. It is something that begins small and *grows through* the moments, the days, and the years of our lives.

So we can live from Monday through Saturday if we trust God's ability toward us and remember our ever-in-process-and-growing faith in Him.

Enduring can be viewed through the lenses of our joy. The battle is God's. He's winning . . . and ultimately we will too! And that thought puts new vigor into enduring. ♥

ABOUT THE AUTHOR

Joyce Landorf is known nationwide as a uniquely gifted Christian communicator, able to convey biblical principles with relevance, humor, compassion, and conviction—in a way that speaks to the needs of men and women in all denominations. A best-selling author of both fiction and nonfiction (her 19 books include *Silent September, Balcony People, Irregular People, He Began with Eve, His Stubborn Love, Mourning Song, I Came to Love You Late, Joseph,* and *Changepoints*), she is also an immensely popular speaker and conference leader. Many may also know her for her nationally syndicated radio program "From the Heart of Joyce Landorf." *His Stubborn Love* film series, based on her nationally acclaimed seminars of the same name, was the recipient of the 1981 President's Award from the Christian Film Distributors Association. Joyce and Dick Landorf reside in Del Mar, California.

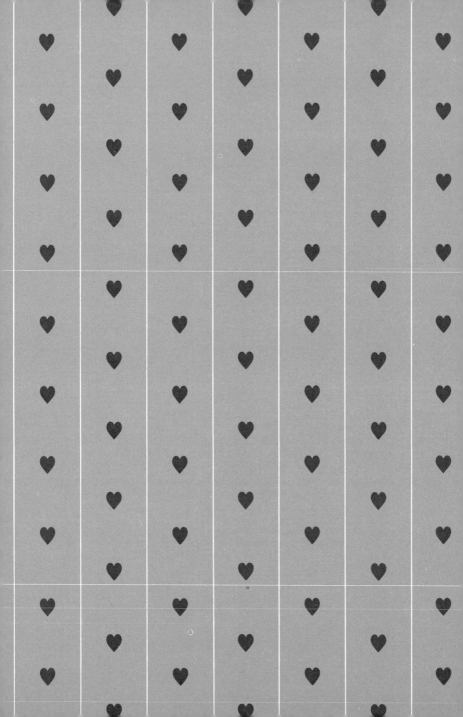